Frustration............................ .... *from Germany?*

"I must confess, I was not familiar with the rules of order of the British Parliament from the 17th century."

Angela Merkel, German Chancellor, 18th March 2019

My good friend Jim Cox sent me a copy of a doctor's note that was provided for Winston Churchill allowing unlimited amounts of alcohol in prohibition America.

January 26th 1932

This is to certify that the post-accident convalescence of the Hon. Winston S Churchill necessitates the use of alcoholic spirits especially at meal times. The quantity is naturally indefinite but the minimum requirements would be 250cc.

This reminded me of my practice in Suffolk. Rather than prescribe antibiotics for a winter cold and cough, I used to advise patients to prepare their own hot toddy and gave them the following prescription:

An inch of whisky

A large teaspoon of honey

Both mixed in either boiling water or hot milk

To be taken before bed

On one occasion, a few weeks later, a patient saw me again and thanked me for the toddy advice, adding "I drank the bottle of whisky doctor, as you advised."

Legal waffle

Sir,
In reference to your report about a judge criticising excessive courtroom deference and legal waffle. I always took it that "with respect" meant "without respect" and "with the greatest respect" meant "listen you idiot". Such archaic wording may have a place after all.

Letter to The Times, 17th December 2018

Sir,
I am reminded of the story of the prolix barrister who, on being told by the judge that what he'd been saying for the past ten minutes had merely gone in one ear and out of the other, retorted "Nothing to stop it, m'lud."

Letter to The Times, 17th December 2018

Pathological poem

Sir

Keats's nine-word line from *Ode to a Nightingale*, "When youth grows pale and spectre-thin and dies", remains the most succinct summary of the demography, signs, symptoms, physical presentation and prognosis of tuberculosis that I have ever found.

Letter to The Times, 3rd August 2019

Optimistic headline spotted in the Loughborough Echo.

Defibrillator installed at crematorium.

4th June 2019

Seen on a chalk-board outside a pub in 2019.

ELECTILE DYSFUNCTION – The inability to be aroused by any of the parties standing for election.

Thanks to Karl Winter

Bad news

Sir

Should the local fox who took my copy of The Times from the entrance to my flat last Saturday, leaving it chewed and strewn in the street, happen to read this, I should like it to know that I am not amused.

Letter to The Times, 14th August 2018

Rural Dangers

Sir

Our Parish Council is so worried by the speed and size of vehicles using the country lanes that it has asked Oxfordshire County Council Highways Department to undertake speed monitoring to assess the danger. Without such monitoring remedial steps cannot be taken. The request has been refused on the grounds that it is too dangerous for their operatives to install.

Letter to The Times, 14th August 2018

I understand the following is often used in educational circles regarding business studies.

The difference between being involved and being committed is as when you have bacon and eggs for breakfast. The hen was involved, but the pig was committed.

Thanks to Neil Doherty

Sensible behaviour

A British submarine, HMS Trenchant, was taking part in a military exercise regarding possible future Arctic warfare. It surfaced through the ice near the North Pole and as there was no evidence of any imminent threat, the crew played cricket.

Thanks to the Forces Network, 20th April 2018

Late in 2018 I received the following email from a good friend, Mark Conroy.

In the days when people actually wrote to newspaper editors, The Times always received more than they could or would wish to print, it must have been refreshing to receive the following letter from a Col. Wintle, writing in 1946 from the Cavalry Club.

Sir

I have just written you a long letter. On reading it over, I have thrown it into the wastepaper basket. Hoping this will meet with your approval.

I am Sir, your obedient servant.

A.D. Wintle

Advice please

The Ashes Test series this year has been remarkable for the run-scoring ability of the Australian batsman Steve Smith.

Christine and I went to Lord's for the second day of the second Ashes Test match.

After we alighted at St John's Wood underground station and were walking along the platform, the announcer on the public address system said "If anyone knows any way of getting Steve Smith out would they please report immediately to the England dressing room".

15th August 2019

Modern absurdities

Sir

In July we were in Padstow and I wanted to book a table for a family birthday lunch. On entering the empty restaurant and enquiring about a booking, I was told, "I am sorry but you will have to ring our booking number. We are in the restaurant business, not the booking business."

Letter to The Times, 8th October 2018

Sir

There appears to be no end to the nonsense of restaurant bookings. In the summer I booked a table at a place with wonderful views across the Channel to the cliffs of France. When the booking was found I was told our table had been booked by another party, that the restaurant was full and that "a reservation was no guarantee of a table."
A risible observation from which the manager would not be moved.

Letter to The Times, 10th October 2018

And one from Devon

An art installation in Exeter consisting of 120 suspended umbrellas had to be dismantled because of heavy rain.

April 2018

The problem with doctors

Frederic Chopin writes to his friend Julien Fontana from Palma:

3rd December 1828

"I have been as sick as a dog for the last fortnight. I had caught cold in spite of the 18 degrees centigrade, the roses, the orange trees, the palms and the fig trees.

Three doctors – the most celebrated on this island – examined me. One of them sniffed at my spittle, another tapped to find where I spat from, the third felt me, listening to how I spat. The first said I was going to die, the second that I was actually dying, the third that I was dead already. I had great difficulty in escaping from their bleedings, vesicatories and pack-sheets, but thanks to Providence, I am myself again. But my illness was unfavourable to the Preludes, which will reach you God knows when.

For the last seven years Wisden Cricketers' Almanack has staged a writing competition. A short piece linked to cricket, of up to 500 words. The prize is publication in the Almanack. I entered this year's competition. I was not successful; I understand it is apparently the taking part that is important. I append my article 'The Price of Lemons' below. Wisden publishes the names of all entrants in the Almanack, which is some consolation even though it has nothing to do with actually playing cricket.

The Price of Lemons

Christine, my wife, and I judge value by the price of lemons. We adopted this as our criterion after over-hearing it while sitting in a Routemaster bus in London many years ago. On seats opposite were an elderly gentleman and a sprightly older lady, apparent strangers and although both English, they started to chat, comparing prices for groceries and fruit. One of them said "I always judge a shop by the price of lemons."

Ever since if we consider something of excellent value we say 'price of lemons'.

My first memory of Test cricket was watching, on the television, Denis Compton sweep to square-leg for four, and England won the 1953 Oval Test and the Ashes. I was seven years old.

The first Test match I attended was England v South Africa at the Oval in 1960. A year later I watched Norman O'Neill score a century in the Ashes Test at the Oval. I still have my ticket from that match, the price was seven shillings and sixpence. Given inflation, that equates to £8.22 today. Over the years since I have kept many of the tickets from Test matches I have attended, and they reveal an intriguing picture.

For Ashes Tests in England, in real terms, the price of a ticket at the Oval essentially doubled between 1985 and 2005 and at Lord's between 1989 and 2013. Tickets today are usually in the £80 - £100 range.

Concerns are often voiced regarding poor attendance at Test matches, although less so in England and particularly less for those at the Oval or Lord's. So, are the ticket prices good value?

They are not dissimilar in cost to a good seat at a West End theatre and compare well with watching Swan Lake at Covent Garden. Watching some of the best theatre or ballet in the world and the finest cricketers.

We were fortunate to be able to watch all five days of the New Year test in Sydney in 1999. On the first day, Australia lost 3 for 52 in 68 minutes, then 5 wickets for 3 runs in the last 15 deliveries, which included a Darren Gough hat-trick. As Wisden reported, the first by an Englishman in an Ashes test since Jack Hearne in 1899.

By 1999 we had both been Surrey members for some years. Surrey had a reciprocal arrangement with Sydney that 100 member's seats would be reserved at each ground for each day of the Ashes tests. We had entered the Surrey ballot and received tickets for all five days in Sydney. We were surprised at our good fortune, not only the allocation of tickets but also being able to watch the match from the members pavilion in Sydney.

Before the match began, we went to the Ticket Office at the SCG, showed our Surrey CCC membership cards and were given our tickets. I asked how much we owed for them and was told there was no charge, as that was the standing agreement between the two grounds. We were delighted and then at the end of the day a hat-trick.
Price of lemons.

Lady Trumpington, the remarkable, able, witty, cigar-smoking grande dame of British politics died on 26th November 2018, aged ninety-five.

When she appeared on TV in 'Have I got news for you' at the age of 90, she commented that she had been asked to sign a form for the BBC to confirm that she was not pregnant.

She contributed to public life in an amazing number of different appointments, from Bletchley Park, to the House of Lord's and as Mayor of Cambridge. When ennobled John Major asked her "Why Trumpington?". She replied that she had only known two places well, "One was called Trumpington and the other Six Mile Bottom, which one would you have chosen?"

On another occasion she said "I wanted to be Lady Fitzbillies, but they wouldn't let me." Fitzbillies is the wonderful cake shop in Trumpington Street, Cambridge.

At the end of 2018 Slightly Foxed celebrated the issue of its 60th edition. In their introduction, the editors, Gail Pirkis and Hazel Wood, shared the following item sent to them by a subscriber, Janet Morgan.

For those of my generation who do not, and cannot, comprehend why Facebook exists: I am trying to make friends outside of Facebook while applying the same principles. Therefore, every day I walk down the street and tell passers-by what I have eaten, how I feel at that moment, what I have done the night before and with whom. I give them pictures of my family, my dog and of me gardening, taking things apart in the garage, watering the lawn, standing in front of landmarks, driving around the town, having lunch, and doing what anybody and everybody does every day. I also listen to their conversations, give them 'thumbs up' and tell them I 'like' them. And it works just like Facebook. I already have four people following me: two police officers, a private investigator and a psychiatrist.

Following the publication last year of 'A Country Doctor's Commonplace Book', I received a letter from the Very Revd Brandon Jackson, a friend from my youth, who I had not seen for about 56 years.
In the interim, he had held the post, amongst others, of Dean of Lincoln. In the book he came across:

Sir
The letters on amusing village names remind me of my favourite graffito. In south Lincolnshire, under the signpost 'To Mavis Enderby and Old Bolingbroke' someone had added 'The gift of a son'.

In his letter Brandon wrote:
When I was in Lincoln, the Dean attended the Bishop's staff meeting as a sort of lateral thinker – at least that is how I defined my role. The Bishop with his archdeacons were daily in contact, running the diocese, whilst I was responsible for the Cathedral, so I often was not very certain as to what they were going on about, especially at the beginning of my time there………..and Miss or Mrs (it had to be one of the other) Mavis Enderby, was frequently on the agenda. It was all rather boring and I was not taking much notice…….and it was before we had started to ordain women – so what was her problem?

The solution came to me by accident. The Rector at that time was Roger Massingberd-Mundy and he had invited me to spend a day with him in his parish and see how remote tiny villages managed to survive. That was when I discovered that Mavis was not a woman at all, but a village, to be added to the growing list of villages for which he had the cure. Here was feudalism still thriving and strong. One of Roger's ancestors had secured the patronage (the right to appoint the incumbent) – hence Roger's role as the Vicar – well, he was vicar of some villages, rector of others. Roger was a delightful character and took not a blind bit of notice of the diocesan rules and regulations , never sought permission to do things, alter or add to any particular piece of church furniture, and never filled out forms…… just carried on regardless and no one in Lincoln knew what was going on down there…………

In 1859 John Murray published Darwin's 'On the Origin of Species'.

When the manuscript was first sent to the publisher, he passed it on to his reader Whitwell Elwin for comments, he wrote back that despite 'the very high opinion' he had of Darwin, he felt the book lacked substance. It would be better, he thought, to concentrate on one species, such as pigeons, 'Everybody is interested in pigeons.'

Murray had the sense to ignore the advice.

The Lake District

Towards the head of these Dales was found a perfect Republic of Shepherds and Agriculturists, among whom the plough of each man was confined to the maintenance of his own family, or to the occasional accommodation of his neighbour. Two or three cows furnished each family with milk and cheese. The chapel was the only edifice that presided over these dwellings, the supreme head of this pure Commonwealth: the members of which existed in the midst of a powerful empire, like an ideal society or an organised community, whose constitution had been imposed and regulated by the mountains which protected it. Neither high-born nobleman, knight, nor esquire was here: but many of these humble sons of the hills had a consciousness that the land, which they had walked over and tilled, had for more than five hundred years been possessed by men of their name and blood........

William Wordsworth. A Guide Through the District of the Lakes in the North of England, 1810

Secrecy

It has been suggested for some years that banks are considering the possibility of replacing personal Pin numbers with fingerprints, because of the potential benefits regarding security in bank transactions.

No doubt a welcome development for those amongst us whose pin numbers have become so secret that we can no longer remember them.

A dangerous British passion

In 2006, 87,000 Britons required hospital attention and treatment after being injured while gardening.

Flowerpots gave rise to 5,300 trips to Accident Departments.

Both Judge and Jury

The following was reported in a wide variety of media on 17th April 2019:

'No, I can't sit on the Jury... I am supposed to be sitting as the judge.'

The resident judge of Winchester and Salisbury has been excused from a stint on jury service after it became clear that he was to be the judge on the same case. At first even that clear breach of the principles of natural justice was not enough. Judge Cutler replied to the Jury summons by pointing out that he was listed to be the judge in the trial but was told that his reason was not a sufficiently strong excuse. He was ordered to contact officials at the Jury Central Summoning Bureau directly.

"I told the Jury Central Summoning Bureau that I thought it would be inappropriate seeing as I happened to be the judge and knew all the papers."

The bureau insisted that even though he was the judge in the case, his appeal for exemption had been rejected. It suggested that Judge Cutler could pursue the matter with the resident judge for Winchester and Salisbury.

He wrote back, saying: "I am the resident judge."

Thanks to James Doherty

Remembering the First World War

A survey of 2,000 people in the United Kingdom at the end of 2018 revealed that:

50% thought that Winston Churchill was the 1914-18 Prime Minister, although 10% suggested that it was Margaret Thatcher.

20% thought we had fought against the French.

Most were aware that an assassination had triggered the outbreak of war, but 6% thought it was JFK.

Asked to name the war's biggest battle, 16% chose Pearl Harbor, 8% Independence Day, 7% the Battle of Hastings, 5% Helm's Deep (from Tolkien's Hobbit books).

Thanks to the SSAFA Charity

John Julius Norwich's Christmas Crackers – a tribute.

His Commonplace selections were published each Christmas from 1970 until last year. A couple of gems:

He came across a correction in a New Jersey newspaper, apologising for an error in an item about a function for foreign-language students at a local university. "Mai Thai Finn is one of the students in the program it said. "We incorrectly listed her as one of the items on the menu."

The Rev. Lord William Cecil was the second son of the Prime Minister Lord Salisbury. Born in 1863, in 1916 he became Bishop of Exeter, where he remained until his death in 1936. There he gained a reputation for eccentricity, thanks to which he was nicknamed "Love in a Mist". When travelling around his diocese (frequently by bicycle) he would often telephone his wife to ask where he was. He kept an excellent chef and a splendid cellar; invitations to the Bishop's Palace were consequently much sought after by Exeter society. The story is told of how at one of his dinner parties the lady sitting next to him saw that she was being passed over by the butler as he served the wine. The following conversation ensued:
"Excuse me, Bishop, but I wonder if I could have a little of your delicious wine? Your butler seems to have forgotten me."
"My dear lady, you must forgive me. Of course – Johnson, please pour my guest some wine at once. But I fear I have a confession to make: I did in fact give orders that you were not to be given wine, since I understood that you were the President of the Temperance League."
"Oh no, Bishop, you are quite mistaken. I am the President of the Chastity League."
"Oh dear, I am so sorry. I knew there was something you didn't do."
Thanks to Artemis Cooper

Henry Kissinger, the former US Secretary of State compared Lord Carrington, who died aged 99 in July 2018.

…….to a "Mozart symphony, bright and entertaining, but with a deeper quality in that he was morally and intellectually faithful to his image."